Order this book online at www.trafford.com
or email orders@trafford.com

Most Trafford titles are also available at major online book retailers.

Printed in the United States of America.

ISBN: 978-1-4907-1826-2 (sc)
ISBN: 978-1-4907-1827-9 (e)

*Trafford rev. 02/27/2014*

 www.trafford.com

**North America & international**
toll-free: 1 888 232 4444 (USA & Canada)
fax: 812 355 4082

# Callula Xu
# Poetry

*Juvenile Poems by*

# CALLULA XU

# Foreword

When I first met Callula Xu she was only nine years old, with an astoundingly grown-up vocabulary and way with words. I learned that she was born in Vancouver, BC, Canada in 2003, and that her parents, with Callula and two older sisters, soon moved back to their homeland of China. When she was four, the family again relocated, first to Vancouver and then to the Bay Area of northern California. Along the way, her parents realized that they had something of a prodigy on their hands. As a very young child, Callula began to read avidly in Chinese and later in English.

Today Callula speaks fluent Mandarin at home and fluent English at her California middle school, where she was recognized as a gifted child and advanced two grades. A story she began working on when she was five was written down in Chinese characters by her mother and sister and published in Chinese with many of Callula's drawings, aided by artist Xiu Juan Ji. In 2013, her second book, *The Adventures of Sir Whittington* (Trafford, 2013), was published with text in both English and Chinese and colorful illustrations by Callula. That book is a charming children's story of a cat (named Sir Whittington) who travels from England to "the New World" and falls in with a tribe of "aboriginal cats" who live in tepees and teach him how to hunt and fish. Written in the form of entries from Sir Whittington's diary, it includes the last will and testament drawn up by that brave cat before going on a dangerous mission. Callula told me in a most adult way that *Sir Whittington* "is not my best work," probably because of its few grammatical slip-ups that any English-speaking kid might make.

This book of poems written at age nine is, I would say, not a children's book at all—though written by that same child. In many poems in the current volume, readers will recognize a juvenile point of view, but her repertoire is far broader than that. She has read widely and deeply in such fantasy tales as J. K. Rowlings's *Harry Potter* series and C. S. Lewis's *Chronicles of Narnia*. They have clearly fueled her impressions of heroic warriors (she is fond of sword-play as well as word-play), of monsters of various degrees of ferocity, and of real and mystical forces of good and evil. She laughs when teased about her "dark side," explaining that images come to her at night as curiosities to be explored rather than nightmares to be feared. She makes up stories based on those images and

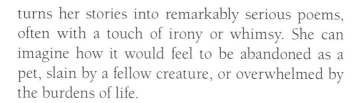

turns her stories into remarkably serious poems, often with a touch of irony or whimsy. She can imagine how it would feel to be abandoned as a pet, slain by a fellow creature, or overwhelmed by the burdens of life.

Despite the heaviness of some of her work, she is anything but morbid herself. She has a pet hamster named Mocha who, she says, goes to sleep when she tries to read poetry to it. She has many stuffed animals and "action figures" which she arranges to act out stories of the kingdoms they inhabit. But beware! One of her favorites is the dog Cerberus, the mythical three-headed guardian of the River Styx. To me, her Cerberus looks more snarly than cuddly, but mostly, she maintains, all he says is "Woof!"

Callula Xu (pronounced like "shoe") is a memorable name. It is definitely a name to remember as she grows up and develops into a mature and skillful poet. That is, unless she gets "muggled" along the way. If you find a flaw in any of these poems, compare them with what *you* were writing when you were nine years old. Enjoy.

*Walter R. Hearn, Ph.D.,*
*Former "Poetry Rejection Editor"*
*of* Radix *magazine.*
*Berkeley, CA; October, 2013*

# Ode to Zephyr

By Callula Xu

Memories.
This blade is living.
Memories of happy times,
Of rising suns and falling deaths.

Now it is quick no longer.
It is still, without a mighty hand to wield it.

NOW.

Tranquil
It lies upon the earth.
Quiet.
The brook caresses it, the merry winds laugh
   Zephyr.

Blade of diamond, flashing through earth.
Head low, the viper strikes, behold the fang
   of woe.
Weaving in, weaving out, Zephyr strikes, a bloody
   trail behind him

He falls, hand to his throat, behold, the
   bloody hero!
He is dying, the millions fall silent, silent with
   respect The battle is won, but the hero is
   forgotten, his name lost in the wind . . .

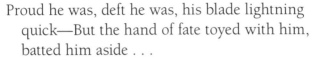

Proud he was, deft he was, his blade lightning
    quick—But the hand of fate toyed with him,
    batted him aside . . .
The hero who brought hope, his blade lives on . . .
Zephyr the bloody, Zephyr the great . . .

# The end to the beginning

### By Callula Xu

The rain falls.
The sky weeps,
Weeping, for what could have been
The end to the beginning.

The courtyard is empty, devoid of life
Bright, tattered strips of cloth hang from the
   walls, A faded banner drags on the ground.
Sad reminders of what once was,
Sad reminders of what could have been.
The end to the beginning.

Some hearts are full with gratitude and joy, and
   bring hope to those around them.
Some hearts are hollow and empty, mourning,
   dying slowly.
Some are old, but their hearts are full, Some are
   young, but their hearts are hollow, Searching,
   searching for what could have been.
There are too many sorrows in this world.
Too many hollow hearts,
Hearts falling apart.
The end to the beginning.

The rain is falling.

## Millions of words

By Callula Xu

Waist deep, in a blizzard.
A blizzard of words.
Trapped, sinking,
QUICKSAND.

A trap, a bog, I fell in,
Waist deep in a pile of words.
Hurled at me, they sting me
They bring tears to my face.
Hurtful, meaningful words,
Designed to make me ache,
To make me hurt, deep down inside
I put on a proud mask every day,
Pretending they can't hurt me
But inside, I cry.
They open up old wounds every day,
Create new ways to hurt
So much I just want to run away
And I cry every night, willing them to heal, To
    heal, and for them to be reopened, Words pour
    salt on my wounds They sting me, they bite me,
    they scratch me, They hurt me.

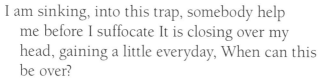

I am sinking, into this trap, somebody help
me before I suffocate It is closing over my
head, gaining a little everyday, When can this
be over?
When can this stop?
Why did they have to create this bog?

Sinking
Into
Their
Trap

# A message for all

By Callula Xu

A little girl put a message in a bottle, And set it
out to sea, Little did she know The reaction it
would bring to many.

A fisherman scooped up the bottle,
Floating in with the daily haul,
Opened the bottle, read the message,
And smiled.
He carefully considered, and threw it back to sea
For others to enjoy, and for others to smile.

There was a cranky old miser,
Whom many compared to a toad,
Walking along the beach shore,
When he found the bottle.
He opened it, read the message,
And a smile came onto his face,
He put the cork back in, and threw it back.

Years later, when the little girl was all grown up,
Walking down the shore, She found the bottle,
Read the crude, knobby words and smiled.

The message who brought joy to others is still
floating today, waiting for you to read it.
So have a merry day to all!

# To start anew

By Callula Xu

My life has collapsed,
Ashes are swept up around me,
I watch helplessly as my life is swept away, I
    regret not having held on tighter, New seeds are
    blown in with the wind, Pushing me forward,
    they take root in my heart, I feel a false sense of
    calm, I relax,

Then, my life collapses,
My dreams blow away with the wind,
Ashes dancing, mocking me,
I reach out, crying 'No!'
A new life sweeps in.
It bumps me and jostles, but takes root in my
    heart, I try to live it to the fullest, Before it falls
    apart,

But this time, it stays.
I've gathered parts of my old life back in, Mixing
    it with my new life and my old old life.
I've learned that an end to an old life
Should be the beginning for a better one.
Once one life is swept away,
It can never be replaced,
But we should make the next one better.

# Greyhound

By Callula Xu

Leap!
Constantly in motion,
Constantly sniffing,
Constantly hearing,
Taking in,
Tracking.

I am the hunter,
Watching,
Stalking,
Always on the alert.
Angry.

Growl.
It is near.
Leap!
Earth rushes through my paws,
Gaining ground,
Almost.

Heart pounding,
Roar!
Dodge and weave,
Almost had it!
Pounce.
Finished.

# Erosion

By Callula Xu

The sculpture resonates.
Hums,
With dark and ancient power.

He was carved into stone.
He looks down,
All-Knowing.
He is solemn.

He is sad.
Grieving.
For what, we don't know.
The reason is lost.

Time eroded him.
Time erased all memories.
Time was cruel to him,
Time left no trace.

He looks down,
Pondering a question lost to us,
He is unknown,
His face set in stone.

His purpose is lost.
We can only guess,
Who he was,
Or might have been.

We are drawn to him,
Drawn to the unknown,
What we would call,
What we could call,
X.

Time has eroded him.

# The true definition

By Callula Xu

She falls, but she will get up.
Unlike some others, she will not pout.
She has stood through rain, and snow, and sleet,
    But she remains proud, Determined.

When she is hurt, she does not sting back, Unlike
    some others, Because she understands the
    definition of humane, Unlike some others.
She will remain true and loyal throughout all her
    days, Showing people That making an effort
    counts.

She has tried her best,
Pushing through never-ending pain,
And has won,
Showing kindness to others,
Forgiving when need be,
But punishing when need be.

This is the ultimate definition.

# Waiting . . .

### By Callula Xu

I am Cinderella the fair,
Waiting for my Prince Charming.
I do wish I'd left a note on those stairs, Instead of
   those accursed glass slippers!
I'm afraid he'll find another Cinderella before me,
   I'm afraid he'll choose one of my stepsisters,
   you see, I think I may just go to him, But what
   will he think of me when we meet?
Maybe he won't like me anymore,
Maybes, maybes, swirling around me.
I see the carriage in the distance!
I must be there, sweeping the floor,
or tending the hearth, smiling a perfect smile,
   He'll see me when he opens the door, I must be
   there!
Oh, I simply can't wait!

# *To Confide*

### By Callula Xu

The young lion was angry at the world.
He was puzzled by its unfairness.
A lion had been shot by a hunter that day.
He went to ask his father, The-One-who-Knows-
    All, Who sighed, lowered his weary but
    majestic head, And confided.

He confided much that day,
so much, in fact,
that the young lion's shoulders drooped with age,
    And he sighed, as he understood the plot of the
    world, Faced the burdens of the world.

When he grew old,
his son was troubled by many things,
So he lowered his head,
And said:

"It is not easy being king when the world is
    against us.
You must have strong shoulders
to bear the burdens of the world,
And even stronger shoulders, to deal with
    your own.
You have only one life,
So live it well,
And make it a life worth living."

# *What we wish*

By Callula Xu

The cat sighs, curling up before the fireplace,
   Dreaming happily of golden days, About the
   days when he'd leapt from roof to roof, From
   rat to rat, Determined that any minute a rat met
   him would be its last.

He was prized, a symbol of glory,
Now faded beyond repair,
I sigh as he curls up on the fireplace,
Dreaming, thinking, wishing,
About my own golden days.

The great ratter is no more,
What chance there was is gone,
And now, we grow old side by side,
Thinking, dreaming, wishing,
That we could go back to our golden days.

# _The stench of fear_

By Callula Xu

The fire leaps.
It stalks me,
THE HUNGRY BEAST

It plays, licking my heels.
I run away.
Something more serious now.
It pounces,
I can smell my fear,
So can the fire.

My heart pounds against my ribcage,
demanding to be let out.
Sweat runs down my face,
I brush my hair back,
ALIVE

I have never felt so alive.
My legs move on, devoid of feeling.
The fire rears up, it is hungry.
It stalks me, hurls me from side to side, I run.

I run, run, run.
I have to run myself into oblivion.
Into that place, of no more pain,
I feel myself being lifted.
I close my eyes.
This is it.

# The Outsider

### By Callula Xu

He is tired of being judged.
He stands, the weary traveler.
He stands alone.

The others are angry,
They laugh and they cry,
Life goes on,
While he stands outside,
But not in him.
He longs for warmth,
To be swept up in the flow,
He stands, alone,
The Outsider.

He cannot warm his hands at any fire but his
    own, For he is the Outsider.
His heart is freezing over.
He cannot warm his heart at any fire but his own.
He made a sacrifice long, long ago,
Trading all he held dear for great power.

But yet, he cannot warm his hands,
Nor his heart,
Nor his soul,
At any fire but his own.
Because he stands in this world as the Outsider.
He is tired of being judged.

# Abandoned hope

### By Callula Xu

The pavement is soaked.
Rain is falling.
Puddles are stepped in.
Unfamiliar yellow rain-boots, occasional
    drenched sneakers.
Strange smells.
Realization.

My owner has abandoned me,
The dog thinks.
He growls at the unfairness,
At the world.
He lies down.
He doesn't understand why.

He is there, day after day, rain or shine.
He is splashed over and over.
He is scorched over and over.
He doesn't understand.
Years later, old and still confused,
He sees his owner come round the corner, To
    get him?
No, with a new dog.

He understands.
He leaps up,
His owner sees him,
Realizes
This was the same dog he abandoned years ago,
    Still waiting.

The dog falls
Into eternal sleep.
Never to rise again.
Innocence is gone.

# Flippin' Pizzas

By Callula Xu

Ten cooks in the kitchen,
Head Cook takes a break.
Joe flips out.
Flippin' pizzas.

Two cooks missing,
Head Cook is mad,
Orders are a-coming in,
Head Cook is feeling BAD!

Hey, Joe!
Yoooooooo?
Whatcha doin'?
Flippin' pizzas.
Where'd you get the dough?
. . .

Four cooks missing,
Head Cook is mad,
Orders are a-coming in,
Head Cook is feeling BAD!

Hey, Joe!
Hiiiiiiii?
Whatcha doin'?
Saucin' pizzas.
Where'd you get the sauce?

. . .

Six cooks missing,
Head Cook is mad,
Orders are a-coming in,
Head Cook is feeling BAD!

Hey, Joe!
Looooooo?
Whatcha doin'?
Cheesin' pizzas,
Where'd you get the cheese?

. . .

Eight cooks missing,
Head Cook is mad,
Orders are a-coming in,
Head Cook is feeling BAD!

Hey, Joe!
Yeahhhhhhhh?
Whatcha doin'?
Bakin' pizzas,
But we don't have—
Joe grabs Head Cook,
Stuffs him in the oven,
No more Head Cook.

I think you know by now, that Joe is mad, And
what he did was really, really bad, But I think
you should feel sad, For the poor customers,
Waiting, unaware, for HUMAN pizzas!

# Lingering

By Callula Xu

Dimly lit,
Reduced to a fraction,
No longer a whole.
Or is this just the beginning?

Smooth walls,
Someone yelling.
Crying.
Pounding.
Coming through,
Vaguely.
Angry words,
Sad words,
Through a veil.
Who is it?

Burnt to ashes,
Crumbling,
A black and sooty husk
Of what it used to be.
Forgetting,
Why?

Drifting,
Lost,
Alone.
Infinity, stretching out before it.
Blackness,
Enclosed.

Lingering,
Dimly remembering,
Wishing that it could remember,
Just once,
Until
Its consciousness
Simply fades away,
Lost forever,
Snuffed out like a candle,
One of many lights that burned out.

It vanishes,
Trying to understand
One thing.
What was it?

# Undead apocalypse

By Callula Xu

Cold
And miserable.
Freezing.
Rain falling,
Unrelenting,
Harsh.

Stumble.
Trip.
Fall.
Aching limbs push on,
Slower and slower,

Pushing,
Aching,
Straining.
Millions are falling.
Millions of those,
Who have gone on before.

Slowly,
Ever so slowly,
Slipping back.
At the back,
Masses of fear
Swept up in the tide,

Falling.
Hit the ground,
Last time.
Breathe out.

The rain is dying.
Everything is dying.
Waves of fear and nausea.
The sun is dying.
The earth is dying.
Among the ruins,
Lost,
Regret.

# Wistful

By Callula Xu

Eating away inside,
Hunger
For power?
No, just something more.
Born to greed.

In a world of greed,
One must want,
For what?
Wanting for something to happen,
For better or for worse.
Just to fight our way up,
Again,
And again,

We lose and we fall.
Our greed consumes us.
We sigh and nod and cry,
We laugh and be mad and ARE.
Nothing, no one can change us.
We can suppress it,
But it will always be there.
Part of us.

We ARE.

# Gone

### By Callula Xu

Sheared away.
In that one second.
Pride,
Dignity,
All gone.

He stepped forward
And spoke
Words of contempt
Scorched into my brain,
Hanging,

Signal of impending doom,
In whatever form I take to hide,
From him, or any one else.
It looms over me,
Burden of the world.

My shoulders sag.
And struggle to keep up.
But they fail,
As always,
And was no more.

# *Emotions*

By Callula Xu

Misery.
Fear.
Hatred.
I feel the emotions of those around me.

They suffocate me,
Smother me,
I want escape.

I had no choice.
So I jumped.
Feeling the wind blow my hair,
Straight up,
Just before I died,
A question came to me.

What of others?
Their joy, their hope, their wishes.
I could live
For that,
But it was too late.
My body plummets,
My soul escapes.
My final thought?

I regret.

# The hero's death

By Callula Xu

Hauntingly vivid.
Vivid, in my mind.
He smiles,
Sad,
Looks on with sorrowful eyes,
Eyes that have seen the sorrows of the world, The
    proud ruler.

Oh, he was mighty,
He was fair,
He was strong.
Icy cold demeanor,
Stoic,
Wise beyond his years.

He stands there,
Hand on hilt,
Cape billowing out in the wind,
He fought many,
Had slain many,
Only to come down at the cruel hands
Of one not worthy.

In no honorable fight
He died,
Without understanding.
At the hands of fatigue,
And exhaustion,
From people calling on him,
Not giving him a moment's rest,
He died a hero's death,
Understanding that heroes are not immortal.

# Abstract Joker

By Callula Xu

Floating,
Serene,
Peaceful,
Silent.

I am the one who watches,
Known and unbeknownst,
The one who calls,
The silent one.

I am quiet,
A stoic surface,
But beneath,
Are turmoil,
Turbulent waters,
Monsters of the mind,
Lurking below the surface.

I am known as a messenger between realms,
    Unpredictable, The Abstract Joker who turns
    the tables.
I read Fate's cards,
And smile or frown,
I had waited for centuries.

The chaos is near.

# Final moments

By Callula Xu

Sparks flew.
Swords clanged.
The bonfire.
Lit up everything.
Illuminating it,
Giving the night a ghostly,
Translucent glow.

Lightning shimmered up and down the length
    of his blade, And as I saw it coming, I knew it
    would be my fate.
So I succumbed.
For the first time I realized.
Nobody thinks of themselves as evil.
To him, he is fighting for justice.
To me, he is my murderer.
Which is it?
Am I real?

As I fell,
I felt naught.
But remembered everything:
My mother's sad, sad smile,
The way my father drank away his sorrows, Not
    caring for the money that slipped down his
    gullet.
The way I fought to live better,

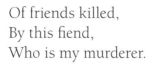

Of friends killed,
By this fiend,
Who is my murderer.

Blinding rage seized me.
So I fought back.
I raised my sword,
And stabbed,
The precise moment in which he pierced my
  heart.
I died
With satisfaction.
With my final, ragged gasps,
I fought back.
He fell off my blade as I fell off his—
And we died.

# *Potential*

By Callula Xu

Rising.
I could see.
For the first time,
I truly saw.
And I repent.

I have seen
And done many horrible things.
I did not know my own wrong,
Until I SAW.

Wisdom
Is not for the wise.
Wisdom is for the fool.
Looking at myself now,
I laugh.
Who is the fool now?
Who is truly wise?

I seek one truth:
What are we?
What can we truly be?

# My Cat

By Callula Xu

You should see my cat's face,
Every morning when I yank open the covers, And
   jump back in, cold feet and all.
I jostle for space,
Squish and push,
And always end up with her on my face.

You should hear my cat purr,
Louder than our car,
Sometimes soft as silk.
At breakfast,
I put out milk
Along with chicken-flavored kibble,
Her favorite.

You should see my cat scratch,
Scratch, scratch, scratch!
I bought her a scratching post,
But she prefers my arms and furniture.
She likes them most.

You should feel my cat's comfort,
Soft and silky and quiet.
Warm in my lap,
I gush over her,
And turn into sap.

You should see my cat climb.
That's all she does.
Climb up into that tree,
Any old tree.
And she won't come down, you see.

I am proud of my cat,
And very proud, at that,
I would never give her up,
No, not for a billion bucks!

# Comforter

By Callula Xu

I bring it down around me.
Soft,
Comforting,
Familiar.

I snuggle,
Feeling my warmth against my skin,
Tingling.
I enjoy.

The warmth of the old quilt spreads over me.
I feel the peace and allow my mind to drift away.
It's soft and familiar,
Has seen me through troubled times,
Always there,
Comforting.
I would be lost without it.

I bathe in the sun,
Cat-like,
Stretching.
Loathe to get up.
I turn
And yawn.
Nap time.

# Who?

By Callula Xu

Darkness.
What is this?
Looking down on myself.
I see an empty shell.

I evoke terror wherever I go,
I can walk, and I am strong
I look almost like a ghoul,
But I am not.

I can clear great distances within one day, And I
    have a strange craving for brains, But what can
    I say?
I feel no pain.
Who am I?
What am I?

# Running

By Callula Xu

All my life
I have been running,
For what, I don't know.
From what, I don't know.
I just run.

Breathe in,
Breathe out.
Despite all this running,
I am actually quite calm.
I am accustomed to it.
I have no family.

Once, I might have.
A fuzzy memory,
Faces looming over me,
Smiling and frowning,
Laughing or crying,
Names, half remembered,
It is painful to try to remember.

Breathe in,
Breathe out.
I am lean and lonely.
The world is harsh.
All that matters to me is running,
It's my only purpose in life.

Breathe in,
Breathe out.

# *Sinner's Plea*

### By Callula Xu

I am afraid
Of many, many things.
Of myself,
Of others,
Of what I have become.

I do not trust easily,
But I trusted It at first glance.
Maybe I felt reckless.
Maybe It compelled me.

It told me many things,
All so childish and hopeful,
Impossible to succeed.
Hinting darker truths,
I believed It.

I bury my head in my hands.
What have I done?
What have I become?
I know, deep down inside,
But I don't want to admit.

I keep on pretending.
I don't know who I am trying to fool.
I am guilty.
I am a sinner.

# Anguish and Misery

By Callula Xu

I am hidden,
Well hidden.
In fact,
No one can see me except my own Kind.

I am the embodiment of many things.
Hunger and Cruelty are my pets,
Obedient beasts,
Though only to me.

Yes, that's right.
I am Misery.
Wherever I walk,
My beasts follow,
Snapping at those who dare to cross the line.
To yield to me is certain death.

No matter how much people try to escape.
I will always be here,
No sense in giving in to me.
Or will I?
After all, I grow weary.
I fear my days are numbered.
But I know one thing.
I will not die without a fight.

I sigh, I moan, I ache.
Once I had Anguish,
To ease my pains.
Anguish went.
And I grew stronger,
Out of my own Misery.

I wish Anguish were here.
I am a cruel lord,
But I know I once was kind.
I gave that up for Anguish,
Whom the Others destroyed.

I miss Anguish.

# Giving up

By Callula Xu

My eyes are so heavy . . .
I want to close my eyes,
Just for a moment . . .
No!
No?

If I close my eyes,
I'll die . . .
It's cold . . .
So cold . . .
Too cold.

Stay awake!
Have to stay awake!
They'll find me soon.
I used to love snow,
Didn't I?
I hate it,
Now that I am trapped in this blizzard.

Curse whoever said snow is beautiful;
Beauty is killing me!
I hate blizzards.
So tired . . .
No! I can't close my eyes!
I'll die!

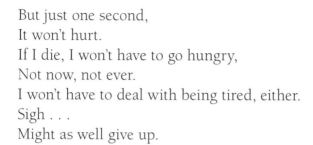

But just one second,
It won't hurt.
If I die, I won't have to go hungry,
Not now, not ever.
I won't have to deal with being tired, either.
Sigh . . .
Might as well give up.

# *Lune*

By Callula Xu

Humming with quiet power,
The tablet is of stone.
Etched into it are records of great deeds and tales,
   If one takes the time.
Imbedded in the center are two hilts, forming
   an 'X'.
I step up. I take the hilts.
I draw.

Suddenly, I am in a different place.
In a different body.
I slash and parry,
Thrust and feint,
With agility and ease not quite my own.
I am Lune.
I disarm my opponent,
Dispatch him with a flick of the wrist.
I survey the battleground,
no Living soul but me left standing,
And say with cold humor, "Next."

I pierced the great boar's heart
Took the head of the evil fiend who called itself
   Wrath, Fighting as a champion, Answering to
   no one and yet everyone.
I am Lune.

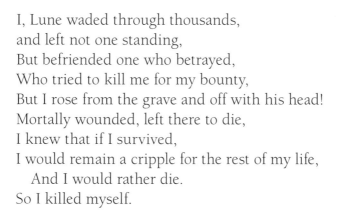

I, Lune waded through thousands,
and left not one standing,
But befriended one who betrayed,
Who tried to kill me for my bounty,
But I rose from the grave and off with his head!
Mortally wounded, left there to die,
I knew that if I survived,
I would remain a cripple for the rest of my life,
    And I would rather die.
So I killed myself.

I came back to the cold room
Where the tablet lies.
The swords are again in the stone,
I bow to Lune,
And exit.

# Marionette

By Callula Xu

Even my bones are aching.
My body is at my limits.
Yet I push on,
Numbing my pain,
A soulless machine.

The blood of thousands stains my soul.
My hands are filthy.
I am a murderer,
Soon to be among the murdered.
I push on,
Knowing that this has to end soon,
But I don't care.

I move with incredible speed,
Darting from one to the other,
Wielding my blade with deadly accuracy.
I finish them off,
Quickly,
Easily.

I am not moving of my own accord.
I do not know what I have become.
I am like a puppet,
Forever dancing,
Only with no strings.

Finally, I fall, grateful to the man who saved me.
I collapse,
And as my blood ebbs out,
I sigh, and close my eyes.
Peace, at last.

# *Hunger*

By Callula Xu

I am The Ravenous One,
With an insatiable appetite.
I devour anything,
Or anyone
Who dares to stand in my way.

I roam this earth,
In search of vengeance.
Scouring this earth,
For anything that stands against.
I have killed millions,
And I do not hesitate.
Thus is your warning.

I have thirsted for centuries,
For the sweetness of human blood,
And soon, I shall walk this earth,
Devouring all that comes my way.

I am the Devourer.

# Claustrophobic

### By Callula Xu

I am trapped.
I have been trapped all my life.
I want to be out in the open.
I didn't used to feel this way.
THEY made me.

Sometimes it gets so bad,
Instead of drawing the quilt snug around me, I
    toss it off, Inviting in the chilly Night.
He is a welcome guest to me.

When they let me out again,
No place is big enough.
I want to see the prairies,
See if they are really never-ending,
And find a place where I belong,
Without any fear.
But I am also half afraid.
If they DO end,
I know I'll waste away.
This dream has sustained me all these years.

I wish I could be free,
Or a clock could rewind.
And let me be a baby again,
And try to redo things as best I can.
But I am stuck,
Here, of all places, too.
THEY must think it's ironic.

Stuck here all alone,
Except for my Claustrophobia.

# The end is near.

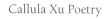

By Callula Xu

Deftly,
I move silently and quickly,
Seen by no one,
A vague, fleeting shadow,
Passing with the wind.

The night is still.
My body pierces the thick night air,
Blade-like,
Slicing through the air.
I shiver.
I look at the tall,
Foreboding building,
Looming over me with ominous presence,
The presence of death.
My end is near.

I scale the wall,
Cat-like,
With all the grace and ease of a panther.
I drop down, silent.
I draw my blade,
And caress it,
Knowing that this would be the end

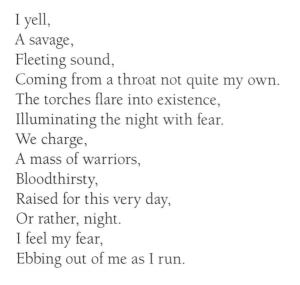

I yell,
A savage,
Fleeting sound,
Coming from a throat not quite my own.
The torches flare into existence,
Illuminating the night with fear.
We charge,
A mass of warriors,
Bloodthirsty,
Raised for this very day,
Or rather, night.
I feel my fear,
Ebbing out of me as I run.

My end is near.

# Kin

By Callula Xu

Moving swiftly,
The winds bring tidings to my ears.
I laugh.
I revel in them.
They sweep me off my feet,
Twirling me,
I am home.
At last.

They carry me,
Aimlessly,
Wandering.
Truly
I am among my kin.

I laugh,
The sound ringing through the air,
Piercing the air.
The winds take me to all sorts of places, Dancing,
    Laughing in their own Silent way.

I am home.
At last.
I have found a place,
A place where I truly belong.
I am content.

# The Hope of thousands

By Callula Xu

Hope is a burden
Meant to enlighten.
Hope is a burden,
Both to those who have it,
Living constantly in fear their Hope will die out,
   And to those who are the Hope.

He was Hope,
Defiant of all others, the Hope of the people,
   Doer of great deeds, protector of all, Slaying
   monsters and men alike, No matter how big
   and tall, no matter how cunning and small.

In a world that was cruel, and heartless, Where
   people just sat and told legends of the heroes of
   old, Wishing, wishing, endless wishing, When
   he came walking out of the sea, A messenger
   from above, and told them all:

I AM YOUR HOPE.

He shouldered all the world's burdens,
And bore it well, but sighed.
People came to him with every little thing, No
   matter how trivial, and he always set it right.
Patient and kind,

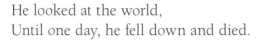

He looked at the world,
Until one day, he fell down and died.

He was their Hope,
The Hope who brought peace to the world
And sacrificed himself
To make the world a better place.
As the Hope of thousands died
The ocean heaved a sigh.
As his life ebbed out like the tide,
The world mourned.

# *Dreamed*

By Callula Xu

Sweat running down my back.
Don't care.
Have to get to the top.
Chances like these are rare.
Have to get up.

Reach, drag, boost,
Good rhythm.
Reach, drag, boost.
Don't look down.
There's a good reason this is called Eagles' Roost.

I think I see the final ledges.
They aren't final.
Now I reach the edge.
Is this it?

Reach, drag, boost.
This is the place.
I'm running out of gas.
Finish this race.
Better do it fast.

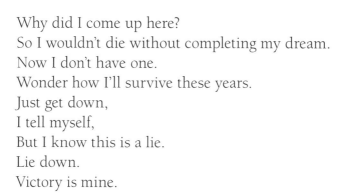

Why did I come up here?
So I wouldn't die without completing my dream.
Now I don't have one.
Wonder how I'll survive these years.
Just get down,
I tell myself,
But I know this is a lie.
Lie down.
Victory is mine.

# Advice

By Callula Xu

Step by step.
Be patient.
It's a long way.
The path is treacherous and full of pits.
If you fall down, get up.
If you fall in a rut, shout for help.
All these words echo in my head.
I have failed them.
What have I done?

I look at myself,
And see
That this rut I have fallen into
Is deep,
With steep walls
And cold reality for the floor,
Which is paved with poverty.
At first, I blamed their advice,
Not wanting to believe I was in here,
But now I know.
Can I get out?

Even my bones ache,
But I am out.
I feel like celebrating.
When I see I am on the edge of a broken bridge.

The waters below are ravenous black depths, The
    yawning chasm uncrossable.
My pride will not let me stop.
Before I know it,
I jump
And I land in a heap.
Bruised and battered, I trudge on.

I look at the grandeur,
The certainty of success ahead of me,
And a curving, steep road.
I look back, and realize that where I have trod, Is
    now straight.
It would be easy to tumble back to poverty.
I run, but I am barely moving uphill
Toward the palace.

Several times shortcuts open up,
But most of the time they are false.
The true ones don't help very much,
But I take them, forcing myself to be grateful.

I am finally here.
I raise my arm,
And with all my remaining strength,
Knock.
The second I touch the door,
I have renewed vigor and strength.
When the door swings open of its own accord, I
    run across the threshold, And find into success.
Their advice was correct.

# *Realization*

By Callula Xu

I clench and unclench my hands.
I study my hands and realize
My existence is irony.

I was blessed with a perfect body
But I maltreated it in search of "Perfect."
I was blessed with my life,
Yet I spent it on useless things.

This amazing body was given to me,
Perfect and healthy,
Willing to do whatever I say.
But I took it and turned it into THIS,
This shuddering mess,
Barely able to take a breath,
Gnarled and hideous.


I feel like my existence is a mistake.
Now, at my deathbed,
I have wronged my days.
Not a single person around me,
Not a single one to say goodbye,
I am truly alone.
I take a shuddering breath, and sigh.
I confront death alone.

# Cycle

### By Callula Xu

The wind reaches out long gentle fingers,
    Yearning to sweep me away with their gales.
The winds are playful,
Chasing each other around trees and filling sails.

The little ship strains with all its might, The wind
    guarding it, Day and night.
The winds and the little ship push on,
And the ocean sends a helpful tide,
But for the people on board,
It's no easy ride.

They stumble off the ship and onto the dock, But
    there's that one person who seems quite odd,
    So they take a closer look and see that he has
    only one sock.
He's clutching a hat tight in one hand,
And his hair is full of sand!
The winds reach out and snatch his hat,
Then they watch laughing as he tries to get it back!

The hat twirls in the wind,
Traveling over the sea
So happy to be free that it's about to sing, When it
    sees land once more and bumps into me!
I barely catch it when the dinner bell rings, And
    then a whole new adventure begins!

# *Secrets*

By Callula Xu

They murmur to each other as they flow through,
　Jostling for rank and some just aloof, Big and
　small, short and tall, Some big enough to burst
　through your roof!
Others are small, compact like a ball,
Or as droopy as a string.
But these are Secrets we're talking about.

When you make a Secret,
Shaping it with your hands,
It curls up in your head and prepares to be told.
If you tell it to someone,
It goes whooshing out of your head
Like a deflating balloon.
If someone else tells you,
It snakes slyly into your ear,
And curls up in your head.
It may not be told for years!

But Secrets are created to be told,
Besides, Secrets are quite bold,
And they worm their way out of your head!
So hold on to your Secrets,
People who have Secret's say,
Why did I want this?
Be warned,
Don't say I didn't tell you.

# *Weaver*

By Callula Xu

I am the Weaver.
The Spinner of Sad Stories,
Teller of Tall Tales,
The mastermind behind all plots.
I tend to every emotion,
Carefully and painfully exact,
Bringing vivid scenes to life.

I was born so long ago that even I cannot
    remember.
For me, there is a beginning,
But never an end.
I have watched,
As the centuries and millennia slip by,
Listened to every dip and rise,
Craggy turns and pleasant rides,
To all the twists and turns there can be in a story.
And I am still listening.
Don't think I'm not here,
Listening.

Many call me the Silent One.
Still more call me the Listener.
But almost none call me by my true name, The
    Weaver.
I bring prosperity and woe.
I can tweak your souls into submission.

You creatures are mostly worthy of telling about,
    And have made admirable efforts.
But never forget that I am here,
And will always be.

I weave the minds of men and women,
Tampering with the children,
I give you stories, both sad and jolly,
And will give you more in years to come, You
    cannot change this.
I will always be superior.

# *Miracles*

### By Callula Xu

They flow beneath my fingers,
Laughing and dancing,
Wailing and bemoaning their sorrows,
Stamping and yelling with rage.
Some even tearing out their
Bushy red beards with every step they take,
  Others sniff indignantly, Floating by, their
  noses in the air, Trying to pretend the others
  aren't there.
I can only watch,
Mesmerized,
As I, as I!
Create these little miracles.

Big, angry ones,
Dismissing you with a haughty word,
Sweet, harmless ones,
Just going on their way.
They twirl around my fingers,
Exploding and shrinking,
Bouncing around,
Pummeling my pencil,
They shriek their way,
Pouring out of my pencil tip,
Squished together,
Trying to get out of that tiny place,

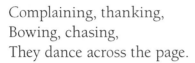

Complaining, thanking,
Bowing, chasing,
They dance across the page.

I don't really control them;
I just let them go.
They're always in my pencil.
There's a good reason why it's hollow.
The lead at the tip has this tiny hole,
Leading to the body
Where thousands of shapes are trying to escape—
    But you can pick which one.
Every morning
I put my pencil into my hand,
Which supplies the shapes,
The pencil is the channel
The shapes spill out onto the paper.

# The creature from the closet

By Callula Xu

Dark.
Hidden.
So well hidden it might be smoke,
Lurking in the shadows.
Every muscle tense,
Drawing taut,
Rigged.

The owner is approaching.
It can smell the scent,
And hear the shuffling footsteps,
Coming to open the door.
Silently, it takes one step forward.
The door knob turns,
Another step forward.
The door is open, just a crack,
Letting in a ray of light.
Another silent step,
Out to the shadow cast by the bed,
Standing still as the door opens wide.

The owner calls out,
And scans the room.
"I know you're there, so get out here!"

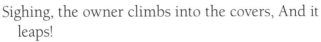

Sighing, the owner climbs into the covers, And it
  leaps!
The owner pulls the covers higher,
Uttering muffled complaints,
But in the end, the dog stays.

# Why?

### By Callula Xu

It shimmers softly,
Catching the light and reflecting it in a bizarre
　　ways, Shifting from shape to shape, So
　　fascinating I feel compelled to stay.
But I can't.

My time, my money, my soul.
Poured into one shimmering sculpture
Which will not last to see the end of the hour.
Years spent,
Carefully planning,
All for this.
I take photographs,
From all sorts of angles,
Mesmerizing by the way it beckons to me, My
　　masterpiece.

I am reckless,
Ruthless,
Merciless,
Unstoppable.
With one wide arc of my arm,
Years go crashing down.
The ice shatters into a million fragments, Flying
　　across the room, I watch as my creation is
　　destroyed, By none other than me.

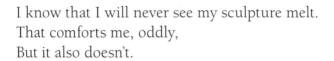

I know that I will never see my sculpture melt.
That comforts me, oddly,
But it also doesn't.

What have I done?

# Life

By Callula Xu

Life blossoms into being.
I can't help it.
Life will come and go with me,
Always so sudden that I cannot predict it.
I have a hard time following it,
But now, looking back,
There are all common traits of life, after all.
Typical, in her nature . . .

Even on the most windless days,
The grass appear to lean towards me,
The flowers sway giddily,
The trees murmur,
Sending shudders coursing through their
    branches.
I give off power.
The type that draws kin to kin,
Life to life.
I can feel the earth pulsing beneath me, If I block
    out the sounds of humankind, and focus.
The rhythm is slow, and steady, and comforting,
    Familiar to me, Calming me no matter how
    alien my surroundings.
Life runs through my veins,
Giving everything a steady, throbbing glow.
I move deliberately,

Thoughts and actions coming to me as fast as
  light.
I move so quickly, so charged with life, The rest of
  the world is in slow motion.

Life lifts me up,
Dancing,
It also forces me down,
And brings uncontrollable rage.
Life is unpredictable,
For that is her nature,
And I am blessed to know,
That wherever I go,
Life will surely blossom.

# The waves

### By Callula Xu

The waves do not wait for anyone.
They are merciless and cruel.
If you devote yourselves to the waves, however,
 You will find that the ocean will reward you
 well, And you will see a side of them never seen
 before, You will rejoice.

If you take care of the ocean,
She in turn,
Will take care of you.
It's not the amount that counts;
It's how you treat her.
Treat her fairly and she will give you justice.
The ocean has no laws,
Because the ocean will be wild,
Until the end of her days,
And to the end of ours.

The ocean runs wild, and does not like to be
 restrained.
She can break free of any bond,
So when faced with an opponent so strong, It is
 advisable to run.

Her waves can be hungry,
Her waves can playful,
Her waves can be mellow.
My warning goes thus:
Treat the ocean well,
Or you will have much to regret.

# Time

## By Callula Xu

Years slip past like minutes,
Now even millennia are seconds,
Mere seconds!
I am old by your standards,
But I am quite young in the universe.
You would know me by a false name,
Old Man Time.

I am here, but not there.
I am there, but not here.
I am many places,
I am also nothing.
I heal your hearts of grief and sorrow
I also steal away your years
I am a concept to you,
Yet I am not merely a concept to others.

You make laws to bind me to your primitive
    minds.
You hasten to restrain me,
To try to tame me.
It is foolish and useless,
For to bind to me,
You would have to understand
That I am not a concept,
But your fear of the unknown restrains you.
I have never seen a sillier,

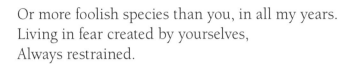

Or more foolish species than you, in all my years.
Living in fear created by yourselves,
Always restrained.

I am Old Man Time to you,
But you cannot grasp the immensity of the
    universe, For you define everything with false
    names.
You struggle to create chaos in the world, But you
    bring in peace much more slowly than chaos.
This is the imbalance,
I predict,
Which will destroy your species.
Finally, a day to look forward to.

# *Blank*

### By Callula Xu

He makes a tempting offer.
The mirrors around us gleam.
I stare just above his head,
Pretending he is a fly,
Buzzing around,
Making annoyed sounds.
He falls silent.
It takes me a moment to realize what he implied.
"I'll be here. In fact, I'll always be here." he says.
He leans across the desk.
"Well?"
I know what I have to do.
"No."
He nods,
Jerkily,
As if he were a puppet.
Forcing a stony smile onto his face,
Snapping his briefcase shut.
He pushes aside a mirror,
And I find myself facing utter darkness, A
    rectangle of utter darkness.
He shoves me inside.
All his fake friendliness is gone.
"Out." He orders.

I walk and I walk and I walk.
There are no walls,

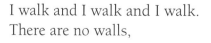

No lights,
Nothing to trip over.
Just me, and the ground I'm walking on.
The emptiness frightens me.
I'm determined not to show it.
Suddenly, there are voices,
Cackling and laughing hysterically.
Eyes appear and disappear everywhere.
A hand touches me,
And I whirl around,
But nothing is there but ghastly heads, Grinning
    grotesquely.
Then I know.
These are the past victims,
Just like me,
I start to run.

I see a faint light ahead,
A wave of hope surges into me.
I run faster,
And faster,
And faster,
And I run myself into the light.
I'm back in the room full of mirrors,
Reflecting the light of the candle in front of me.
So everything is bright.
Too bright.
I notice a change in scenery.
This time,
I'm the one sitting at the desk,
And he's in front of me.
I smile.

# *Phantom call*

### By Callula Xu

It echoed across the water,
Long,
High,
Keening,
A desperate scream.

The birds took flight,
In flocks of multicolored streaks.
Light filtered in through the window,
Gray and desolate.
How odd their sudden color was.
I raise my head,
Tugging weakly on my bonds,
And to my surprise,
They broke.
For the first time,
I had seen color.

I hurried down the hallway.
The guards were enraptured by the desperate,
    keening song, And as I stepped outside, I saw
    color again.
But as soon as I moved towards it,
It stopped.
So did my heart.
I never knew what hit me.

# Traitors

By Callula Xu

Cursed as a fox, I can only wait, and see.
I watch from the shadows,
Cursing my years,
My dull,
Endless years of waiting.
Other demons come and go,
Ghastly creatures,
Trying their luck.
At a mystery they can't solve,
Because they will never understand my grief.

Some demons stop by,
To console me
And to advise me
Others shun me,
Deliberately,
Because I am unwelcome even to my own kind, A
    traitor in their midst.

I am one who watches,
Slinking from shadow to shadow,
My coat agitated by betrayals
That twitch and pop.
So many burrs lodged in my hide,
Weighing me down,
As if each step is an axe in my side.

I am unwelcome.
I know it is true,
Because I can sense it,
Just as I can sense when a betrayal is coming.
Hurtling, breathtakingly fast,
Wickedly, my fate comes to me,
Slicing through the air,
Which is thick with remorse.
I register my shock,
As it lodges in my coat—
And pierces my heart.

# The game

By Callula Xu

There are two options in the game.
This game is not easy, nor is it hard.
Often, it is not fair,
But when it is, it will not shift in your balance, At
    least not as often as it seems to slip toward you
    enemies.
It is full of ups and downs,
But that's what makes it worth playing.

I play this game with everyone I meet.
They are excited or bored,
Watching with fascination as I cast the die.
Bouncing to a stop,
It declares the odds,
Sometimes I think the casting is the most
    important of all.

I love the feeling of the die in my palm, Opening
    my hand and watching it balance, Delicately on
    my fingertips, Rolling off and landing.

There will always be at least two choices.
Many are crushed by the responsibility, But more
    often they don't see the other way out, The
    other option.

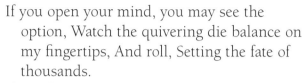
If you open your mind, you may see the
option, Watch the quivering die balance on
my fingertips, And roll, Setting the fate of
thousands.
If you feel like a quick game,
Come to me.
I'll show you the two choices of life.

# *Nothingness*

By Callula Xu

I watch as it moves a piece.
An exquisite heart-play,
But not good enough.
"No can do."
I remind,
Gently,
Suppressing my sorrow.
It is moody today,
Balky and skittish and who knows what else, As
    stormy as the clouds ahead.

I raise my head as the first patters of rain fall,
    Bouncing gently across the stone, Skipping,
    Skidding, Twirling in the air.
The fog drifts aimlessly,
Hanging
Like an unpleasant reminder,
Which it is.

Suddenly,
I am back.
Back to that day,
When I was still mortal,
Tempted by offers, snatches,
Glimpses into immortality.

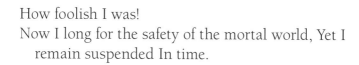

How foolish I was!
Now I long for the safety of the mortal world, Yet I
    remain suspended In time.

I know nothing.
Nothing,
Of what put me here,
Of what I have done to deserve its wrath.
I just sit placidly,
And watch as my visitors
Come
And go . . .

# *Bottles*

By Callula Xu

There is a bottle.
In fact,
There is one for everybody
In the entire world!
Even the babies.
And the animals.
Some are full.
Some are not.

These bottles contain your life.
They're stored in a big, musty storage.
Lined with shelves and shelves.
And balancing precariously on those ledges?
Those are the bottles.
If you carefully uncork the cork,
And leave the bottle out in the sun
The life inside,
Knowing nothing but dark and damp,
Will seek the sudden,
New light.
Curling tendrils of silver mist,
Probing tentatively into the air,
Feel the warmth,
The breezes,
And evaporate.

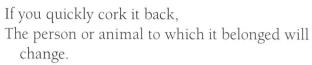

If you quickly cork it back,
The person or animal to which it belonged will
    change.
No longer sane.
This is because it has felt the horrible feeling,
    When part of your life source has floated away,
    Leaving a dim memory And scars on your soul.
Scars that throb when pain is foretold.

If you shake a bottle,
Only a bit,
The life in question gets deathly sick.
If the bottle shatters,
The life will blow away with the wind.
That's how fragile life is.

# Nightmare

By Callula Xu

Running.
No idea how I got here,
Or where I am,
Or who I am—
For that matter.

Chased.
No idea why.
Don't know what's chasing.
Sneak a peek over my shoulder,
See empty air.
Instincts tell me not to stop.

Ice-cold claws rake my shoulder.
Fear tightens its icy grip around my heart As
    fangs snap closed, Where I had been, Just a
    second ago.

Then I know.
The thing chasing me
Was sired by Death and Fear,
Something of the Dark,
A creature made to kill.
An abyss looms up ahead of me,
Smelling of blood and fear.
I know this will be where I face it,
So I turn around.

My heart nearly stops.
The creature has fangs,
Terrible and stained with blood.
Its gleaming eyes are red,
Full of hatred.
A cry echoes up from the abyss,
Hauntingly ringing in my ears.
The creature charges,
But I step aside,
Watching with horror,
As it falls into the abyss,
Twisting and snapping in the air,
Howling.

I shudder.
I find I'm in my bed.
The covers are sweaty and tangled,
But I'm alive.
I breathe a sigh of relief,
But then I hear it growl.
Slowly,
I turn my head,
And find it crouched in the shadows,
Growling.
It followed me here.

# *Deals*

By Callula Xu

All things have a weak point.
You just have to find 'em.
I'm good at that.
Real good.

With the right tools,
I can make you hallucinate,
The bravest man becomes a meek, frightened
   sheep.
You just have to take that bait.
And remember: what they sow, you shall reap.

Know exactly which buttons to push.
Don't say anything,
Don't rush,

Make some good deals,
Such as living filthy rich for the rest of your days.
Or Immortality elixirs,
To keep deadly diseases at bay.
Or Wealth and Power—
But they have to go hand in hand;
You can't have one without the other.

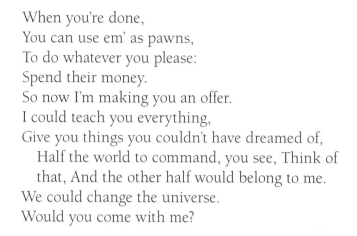

When you're done,
You can use em' as pawns,
To do whatever you please:
Spend their money.
So now I'm making you an offer.
I could teach you everything,
Give you things you couldn't have dreamed of,
    Half the world to command, you see, Think of
    that, And the other half would belong to me.
We could change the universe.
Would you come with me?

# *Bizarre*

By Callula Xu

The universe is shaped like a pear.
Soccer balls grow on trees.
Gigantic man-eating slugs are everywhere.
Trees can fly,
Dust balls are severe menaces,
And all the squirrels are tie-dyed.

Who knows?
The continents change shape every day,
A sleeping man found himself speared on a
   mountain.
This world is bizarre in every way.
If you're nice to the clouds, maybe they'll give
   you rain.
Who knows?

Nine cockroaches in the entire world,
Each one weighing at least a ton,
Even though they're smaller than your
   pinky's nail.
Besides, your ears are bigger than the sun.
And on balconies there are no rails.
Bizarre.

This world is bizarre.
Bizarre,
Bizarre,
BIZARRE!

# Complaints

By Callula Xu

Famine rides the land
On his skeletal,
Crazed,
Starved, and bony hat-rack he calls a horse.
I'm thinking about using it as a toothpick.
He charges,
And falls off his stupid beast.
Where he lands,
Famine spreads.

Misery just sits there and makes more misery.
He used to be better,
But now that Anguish is gone,
He has lost his purpose.
His beasts are worried.
They are afraid,
I am afraid—
That one day he will fall asleep,
And when he wakes,
He will be nothing more than a shell.

Malady is brainless.
He just likes showing off,
And trying to make us jealous.
He wants more glory,
A cult, wealth,
Which we have granted,

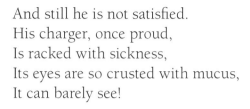

And still he is not satisfied.
His charger, once proud,
Is racked with sickness,
Its eyes are so crusted with mucus,
It can barely see!

And don't get me started on Tragedy,
Most of all,
Because that's me!

# *Spring*

By Callula Xu

The willow trees murmur to the stream,
Who giggles,
Tickled by the leaves.
The stream trickles through the forest
Of tall and solemn pines,
Frowning down at frivolity,
But secretly laughing inside.

The birds cheep softly from overhead:
Greetings,
Updates on hatchlings,
The newest place to find some worms
That something new is in the air,

The squirrels laugh,
Jumping nimbly from tree to tree,
Saying one thing.
Just one thing.

It's SPRING!

# Truth

By Callula Xu

Deceiver.
Trickster.
Traitor

Three fancy words for one thing:
Liar.

We labor on this earth,
Leading lives as deceivers,
Using trickery,
Hoping to stave off death for one more day, We
    are betrayers, Wanting some meager coin
      For gain.
Every one of us is a traitor.

Animals know better.
Dogs are loyal to one who treats them kindly.
Steadfastly by your side.
Humans backstab and hunt their own kind.

Wolves have never eaten their own kind.
We are insane enough to try.
We misinterpret,
Blindly hacking,
Flailing,

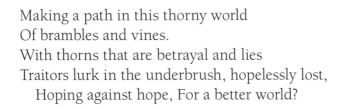

Making a path in this thorny world
Of brambles and vines.
With thorns that are betrayal and lies
Traitors lurk in the underbrush, hopelessly lost,
 Hoping against hope, For a better world?

# *Endings*

### By Callula Xu

As a starving man draws his last breath, He
    thinks of food, Comfort, Warmth, Of all things
    good— And he lets them go.

When the people find him,
In the morning,
They find a corpse,
Sitting at the corner of the street,
An eerie smile on his face.

They speculate.
Shake their heads,
Murmur "Poor man,"
And walk away.
This is the nature of the world.

# *Release*

By Callula Xu

The wind brings familiar scents to my nose:
The briny tang, the kelp,
The seagulls screeching,
Wheeling,
Wheeling overhead.
But today, the saltiness on the winds
Smell more like the copper-taste of blood.

The wind tugs at my scarf,
At my hat,
At my baggy clothes,
As I carefully make my way down the pebbly
    slope, Avoiding the jutting rocks.
The urn seems very, very heavy,
As if I was carrying the weight of the world.
Or maybe,
Just my heart.

I carefully open the urn,
Holding it up to the wind,
Pouring gently,
But before they get to the sand,
The ashes are snatched up by the wind,
Twirling in its long fingers.
Today,
Of all days,
I welcome the sea.

# *Power*

### By Callula Xu

The earth is rich and soft,
Damp, full of life,
Fertile,
Warm.

Cupping the dirt in my hands,
I feel its power.

But here the ground is sun-baked.
Parched.
I tip my water flask and watch,
As the last drops of my water slip away.
They quickly disappears,
Consumed by the ravenous earth.

I press my hands against the ground,
Drinking in its warmth,
Relieving it of the endless heat, if only for a
    moment.
Power wraps tendrils around my arms,
Slowly going up.

Here the ground is hard and cold,
Full of pebbles,
Just grit, and useless efforts.

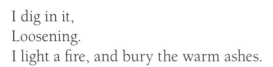

I dig in it,
Loosening.
I light a fire, and bury the warm ashes.

I kneel,
Placing my forehead against the earth.
And give it warmth,
Power,
All I have.

I feel the ground humming,
Pleased beneath my feet,
It will obey.

# Fog of blood

By Callula Xu

I slash out, blindly,
Forcing all my strength into this one blow, Trying
    to separate the fog, but I lose my balance,
    and fall.
I drive my shoulder into the ground,
Sliding a couple of inches.
Suddenly, I can see,
Can hear war cries,
See the carnage around me, but something is
    wrong.

The fog presses down on me,
Swirls around, and I realize,
I am at the eye of a hurricane.
Except, this fog is made of blood.
Seeping into my skin,
Driving blunt lances into my chest,
It sends me backwards onto a spear point.

I roll.
I twist in mid-air,
And the spear opens my eyes.
Piercing my shoulder,
Sending a stream of blood out into the fog.
My blood hungrily devoured.
I can see.

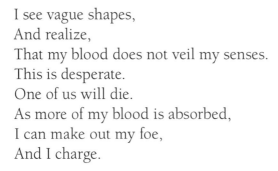

I see vague shapes,
And realize,
That my blood does not veil my senses.
This is desperate.
One of us will die.
As more of my blood is absorbed,
I can make out my foe,
And I charge.

# *Mute*

By Callula Xu

The blood pours out of my wrist,
Bright red,
Human.
What have I done?

All my life
I lived in silence.
I felt like a stranger in my own life,
Looking down at somebody,
That couldn't be me.
Feeling no pain,
No joy,
No grief.
Just dull sensations,
Coming through a veil,
Blurring my senses.

I did not feel consequences.
I did crazy stunts.
People always gaped,
And screamed,
Overreactive.
Or so I thought.

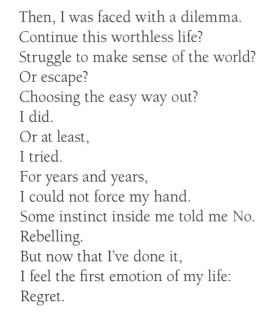

Then, I was faced with a dilemma.
Continue this worthless life?
Struggle to make sense of the world?
Or escape?
Choosing the easy way out?
I did.
Or at least,
I tried.
For years and years,
I could not force my hand.
Some instinct inside me told me No.
Rebelling.
But now that I've done it,
I feel the first emotion of my life:
Regret.

# Chain

### By Callula Xu

The blade of grass waved with its brethren.
This was the life,
With the warmth of the sun and the whisper
   of the rain, Nutrients of the soil warming it's
   roots, And also the tickling of the wind.
But then the rabbit came.

One quick hop and the rabbit was out of his nest.
Sniffing, swiveling his ears to the wind, Detecting
   ordinary Nighttime sounds.
He began to munch.
The wind ruffled his fur.
The grass crunched beneath his paws.
One last snack,
And he would be done.
Back to the bushes,
Back to his den,
Just this one last blade of grass—
Then he'd be done.
Little did he know that minute would be his last.

The hawk dove,
Talons outstretched,
Raking the rabbit's back.
The rabbit turned to run
As the hawk plunged,
Hurtling through the air,

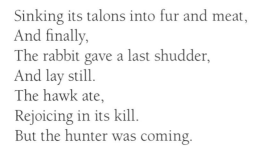

Sinking its talons into fur and meat,
And finally,
The rabbit gave a last shudder,
And lay still.
The hawk ate,
Rejoicing in its kill.
But the hunter was coming.

The hunter watched as it wheeled the sky,
    Screaming it's triumphant cry, Waited for the
    hawk to swoop, And shot.
The hawk, hit in the wing.
Went down
Wing askew,
Plummeting to its death.
The hunter pursued,
But all was for naught.

Finally, the hunter gave up.
The hawk lay shuddering,
Bleeding in the grass.
It tried to fly—
With rattling gasps,
Let out its last.

The grass bowed solemnly,
Thanking the provider,
Taking in nutrients absorbed from the hawk,
    Taking in the sun, The moon, and the wind.
They will not tell.

# Rag doll

By Callula Xu

When we got it,
It was obviously used.
One eye was gone,
The hair uneven,
One arm hung loosely,
By a thread.

Still, we gave it a home,
Fed it, clothed it,
Never gave it any but the best,
Best that we had—
But that wasn't enough.

It was gone,
When I woke up this morning.
Usually,
It would be snug in my arms,
Smiling that half smile.

Later I found a note.

It said it was tired of pretending that it was happy.
It hated us,
Hated everything.
It thought it deserved better.

So now it comes back,
With only one arm,
The bad one,
And no eyes.
It asked us to take it back,
Into our home,
Into our lives.
Into our good graces.

We said no.

# *Spoils of war*

By Callula Xu

I gaze up,
At the sky,
So clear!

I hear weak cries around me,
The last moans of a dying man,
The pain in my stomach vanishing.
Another corpse is tossed on top of me,
Heel hitting my stomach,
And pain brings me back.

I lie there,
As helpless as a gutted fish,
Some dead man's dirty boot in my open wound.
It seems just yesterday when I enlisted, The man
   behind the desk laughing, Making jokes about
   my youth.
He asked me,
Did I want to throw my life away?

I said yes.
For my country.
Noble words,
But hollow.

The sky is blue.
Soon I'll leave this world,
Rid myself of pain . . .
There is a tunnel.
Mother . . .
I raise my hand.
No!
Where are you going?
Mother!
Don't leave me!
Don't . . . .

# Gray

### By Callula Xu

The days are dull.
The sky outside should be blue,
Children running underneath,
Arms up,
Jumping into piles of leaves.

But sitting here,
My world is gray.
Painted with shades of black,
Dark grays,
Dull grays.
I am doomed to sit out the rest of my days.

I twist on the hard little footstool,
Wincing as the harsh squeak escapes,
Propping my elbow on my knee,
And my face in my hand.

I am alive.

Yet, I have died.

I do not know why.

# Gallop

By Callula Xu

The grass is sweet.
The sun shines,
Warming my coat.
I want to run.

So I do.

The herd is moving,
Surging forward,
Generations upon generations of life,
Slipping through our hooves.
Wild,
Untamed,
Uncontrollable.

We are channels of that power.
It visits us,
Pouring into the ground,
The air alive around us.
We run.

The steady rhythm of our hooves is soothing,
　　Propelling ourselves forward, Faster and faster,
　　Until we are not quite real.
We are powered by the wind.

Soon,
Too soon for my liking, we stop.
Graze a bit, sleep a little,
Doze off.